Starting school

This book belongs to

....

Colour the star when
you complete a page.
See how far you've come!

Author: Carol Medcalf

How to use this book

This book is designed to help your child become better prepared for school and can be used during the reception year. It focuses on all seven areas of development required in school, increasing in difficulty as your child works through the book to challenge and extend their knowledge and skills.

- Find a quiet, comfortable place to work, away from distractions.

- Activities in each subject get harder as you work through the book, so work through in order, spending time on suggested further activities before moving on.

- Help with reading the instructions where necessary and ensure that your child understands what to do.

- When questions have two parts, it is often best to gain the first answer and record it before moving on to the next part of the question.

- If an activity is too difficult for your child then do more of our suggested practical activities (see Learning tip) and return to the page when you know that they're likely to achieve it.

- Always end each activity before your child gets tired so that they will be eager to return next time. Judge their mood carefully to make this a positive experience. Learning should be fun and not forced.

- Help and encourage your child to check their own answers as they complete each activity. If your child gives an incorrect answer, try to avoid saying that it is wrong. Instead ask them to check their own answer carefully so they spot the mistake.

- Let your child return to their favourite pages once they have been completed. Talk about the activities they enjoyed and what they have learnt.

Special features of this book:

- **Learning tip:** situated at the bottom of every left-hand page, this suggests further activities and encourages discussion about what your child has learnt.

- **Progress panel:** situated at the bottom of every right-hand page, the smiley faces help your child to process how they feel about the page and their achievements.

  Here's a key to help explain what the faces represent:

  🙁 I feel uncertain/I don't understand yet

  😐 I feel OK/I need more practice

  🙂 I feel happy/I fully understand

  It is important that they are building confidence in their abilities and feel good about themselves.

- **Certificate:** the certificate on the inside back cover should be used to reward your child for their effort and achievement. Remember to give them plenty of praise and encouragement, regardless of how they do.

All the activities in this book reflect the goals of the Department of Education's 'Development Matters in the Early Years Foundation Stage (EYFS)'. Your child's nursery or school will be teaching the subjects found in the seven areas of learning and development of the EYFS.

This table shows which pages of this book focus on which areas of learning and development:

Area of Learning and Development	Aspect	Pages
Personal, Social and Emotional Development	Making relationships	Pages 4, 5
	Self-confidence and self-awareness	
	Managing feelings and behaviour	
Physical Development	Moving and handling	Pages 6–9
	Health and self-care	
Communication and Language	Listening and attention	Pages 10, 11
	Understanding	
	Speaking	
Literacy	Reading	Pages 12–15
	Writing	
Mathematics	Numbers	Pages 16–19
	Shape, space and measure	
Understanding the World	People and communities	Pages 20–27
	The world	
	Technology	
Expressive Arts and Design	Exploring and using media and materials	Pages 28–31
	Being imaginative	

Published by Collins
An imprint of HarperCollins*Publishers* Ltd
The News Building
1 London Bridge Street
London SE1 9GF

HarperCollins*Publishers*
Macken House, 39/40 Mayor Street Upper,
Dublin 1, D01 C9W8, Ireland

Browse the complete Collins catalogue at collins.co.uk

16

ISBN 978-0-00-815159-1

The author asserts the moral right to be identified as the author of this work.

British Library Cataloguing in Publication Data.

A Catalogue record for this publication is available from the British Library.

Written by Carol Medcalf
Page layout by Contentra Technologies Ltd
Illustrated by Contentra Technologies Ltd and Jenny Tulip
Cover design by Sarah Duxbury and Amparo Barrera
Project managed by Chantal Peacock, Sonia Dawkins and Tracey Cowell
All images ©Shutterstock.com and ©HarperCollins*Publishers*
Printed and bound in the UK

MIX
Paper | Supporting responsible forestry
FSC™ C007454
www.fsc.org

Contents

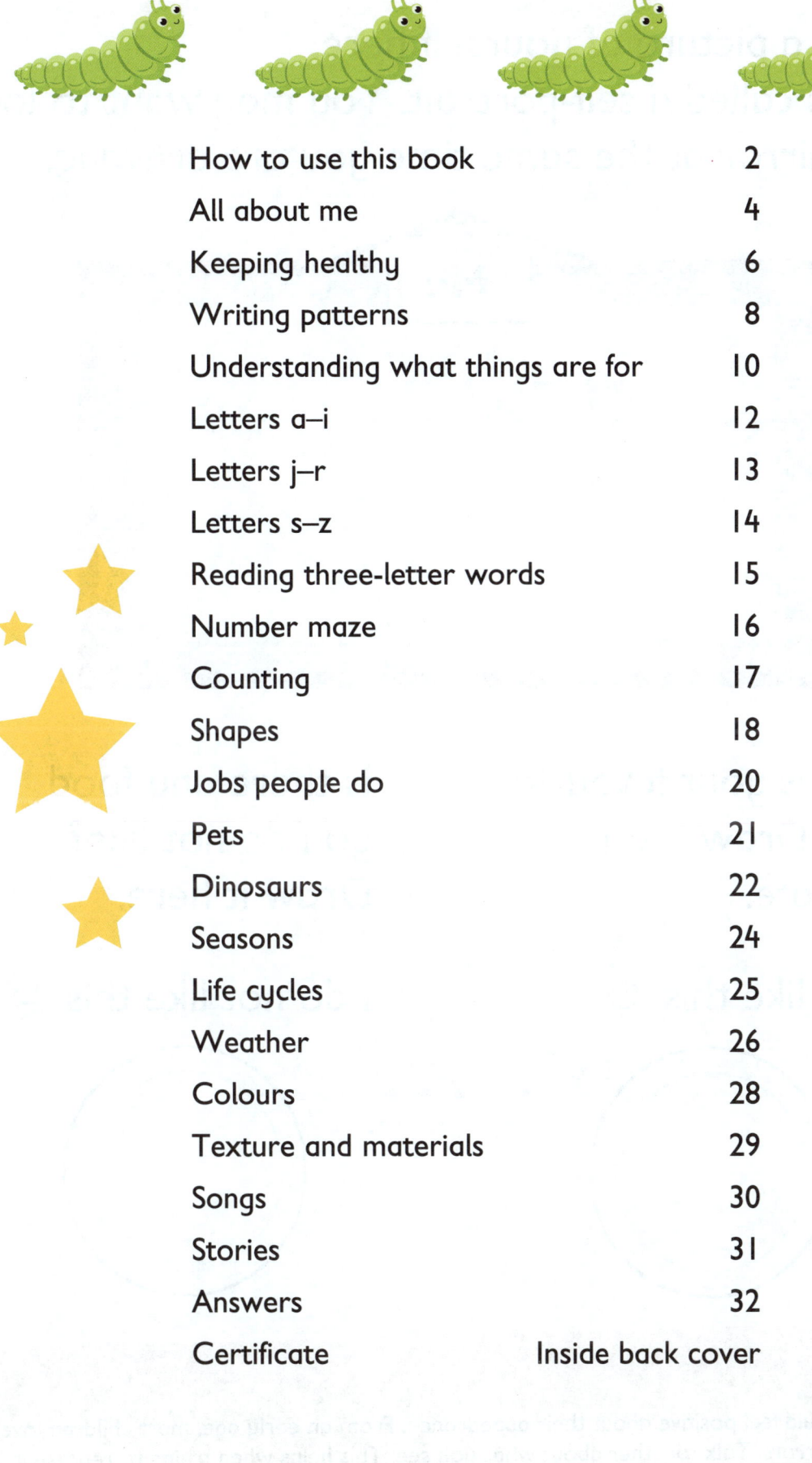

All about me

- Draw a picture of yourself here.
  This is called a self-portrait. You may want to look in a mirror at the same time you are drawing.

- What is your favourite food? Draw it on this plate.

I like this

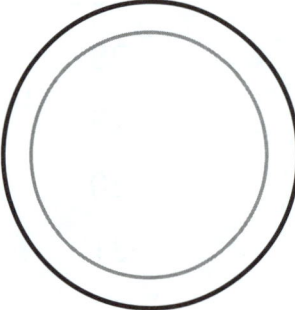

- Is there any food you do not like? Draw it here.

I do not like this

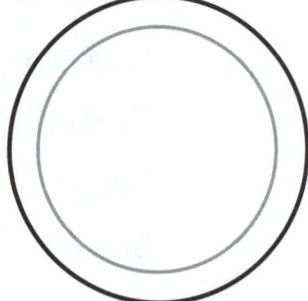

Children should feel positive about their appearance. From an early age, most children love looking in mirrors. Talk together about what you see. This helps when trying to represent themselves through drawing.

● Can you draw your family here? You may want to include pets too, if you have any.

My family

● Complete the picture gallery by drawing a picture of your home.

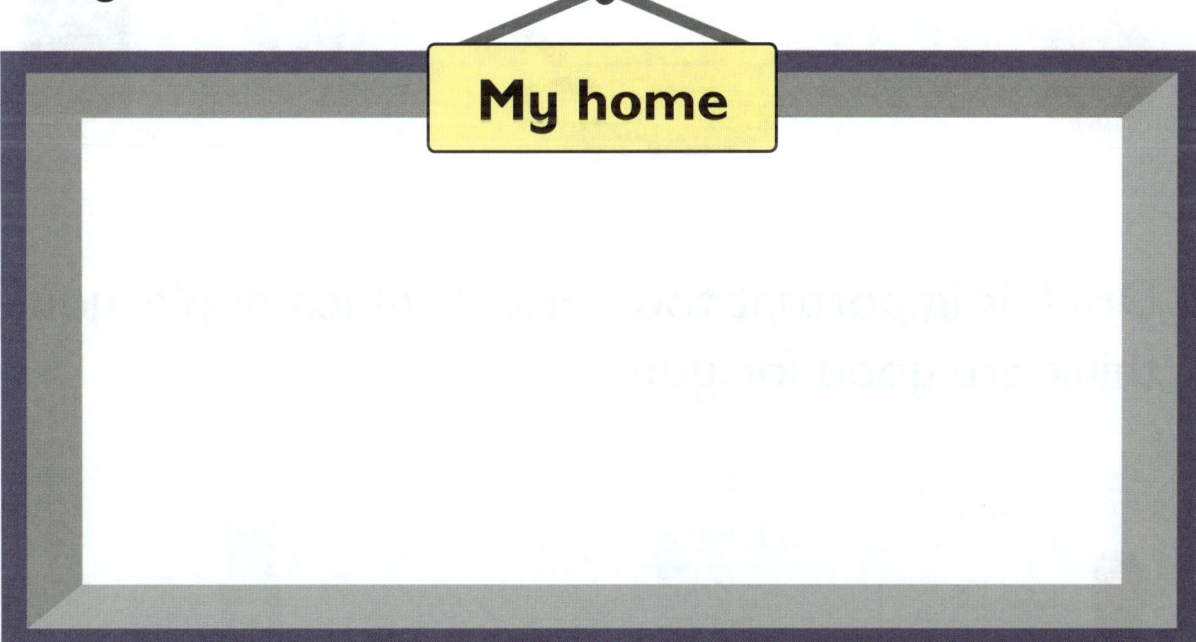

My home

How do you feel about these pages? Tick ✔ the box next to the face that shows how you feel.

 ☐   ☐   ☐

Keeping healthy

We need to eat different types of food for our bodies to grow and stay healthy.

- Circle all the things that are good for you to eat.

- Drink is important too. Tick ✔ which drinks you think are good for you.

Eating habits that are formed in early childhood are likely to last children throughout their lives. At this age they can learn what is good for them and what is not. It is important for them to know they can eat unhealthy foods sometimes, but need to eat different types of food to make a balanced diet.

We also need exercise to keep us fit.

● Can you tick ✔ which of these activities you do often?

walk	cycle	run	climb	stairs

☐ ☐ ☐ ☐ ☐

● Below are some pictures of other things that keep you healthy, and some that don't. Can you put a cross through the pictures that are **not** healthy?

How do you feel about these pages? Tick ✔ the box next to the face that shows how you feel.

 ☐ ☐ ☐

Writing patterns

● Join the dots on the eggs to make the patterns. Colour to decorate the eggs.

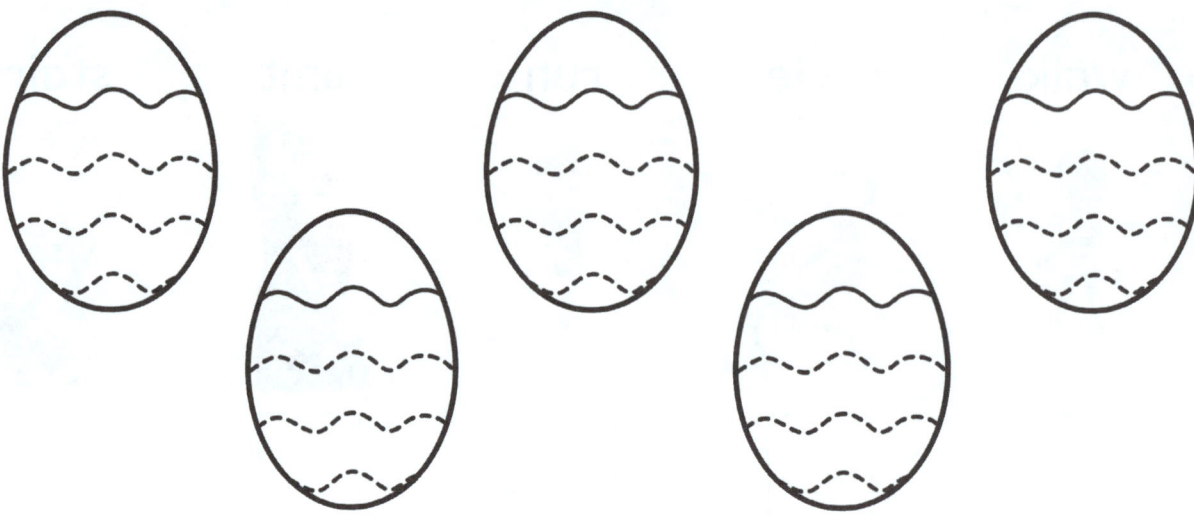

● Start at the red dot. Can you join the dots to help these chicks get back to the hen house?

- Use a pencil to trace over the lines to draw the picture below.
Colour the picture.

How do you feel about these pages? Tick ✔ the box next to the face that shows how you feel.

 ☐ ☐ ☐

Understanding what things are for

- Draw lines to match the actions with the objects. What would you use to…

write

cut paper

cut wood

make tea

make a car go

When doing practical things around the home, talk your child through what you are doing. Perhaps say things like 'Oh, I have forgotten what I need to put this card in to post it. I need an... envelope'. Don't take it for granted they always know what is needed to make things happen.

Draw lines to put these objects in the correct rooms.

Spot the things that are not in the correct rooms. Circle them as you find them.

Letters a-i

● Draw lines to match these letters to the picture that starts with the same sound.

a
b
c
d
e
f
g
h
i

Talk together about what letter things start with. Try not to test, rather say, 'I wonder what letter this would begin with…I think it is 'a'".

Letters j-r

- Match these letter sounds to the correct picture.

j

k

l

m

n

o

p

q

r

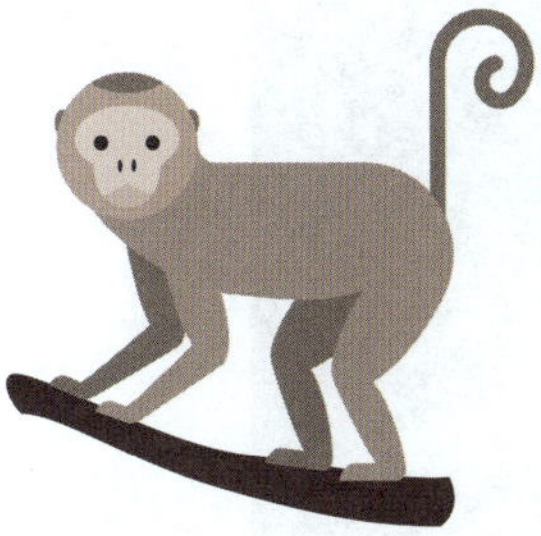

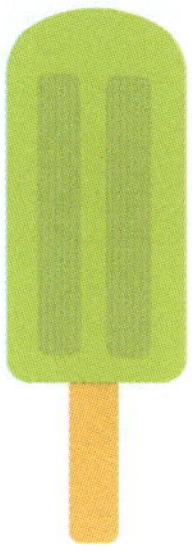

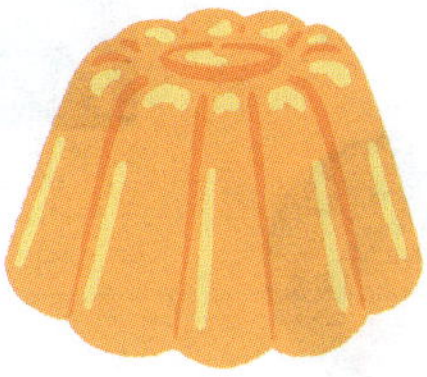

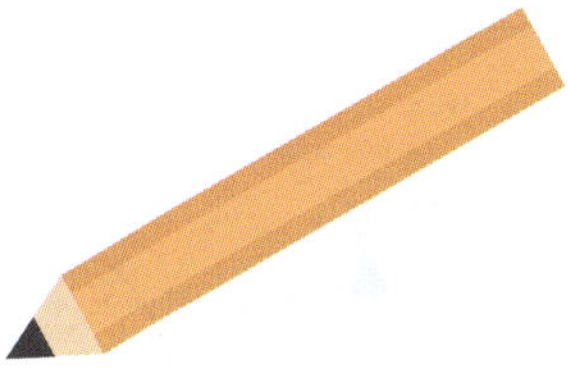

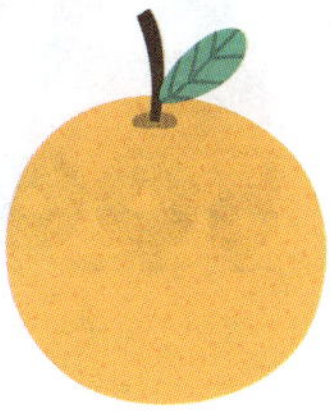

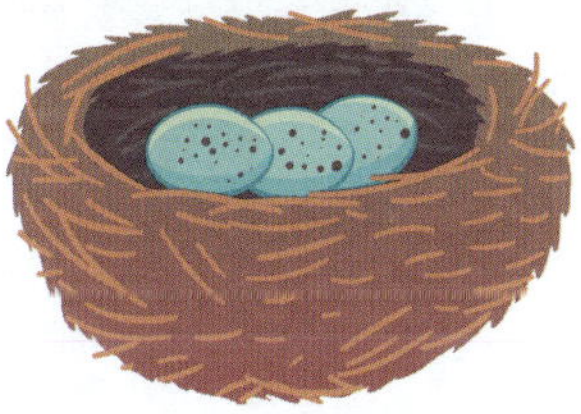

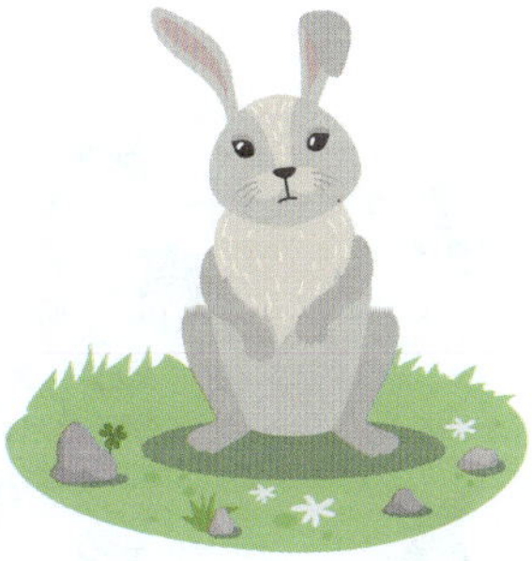

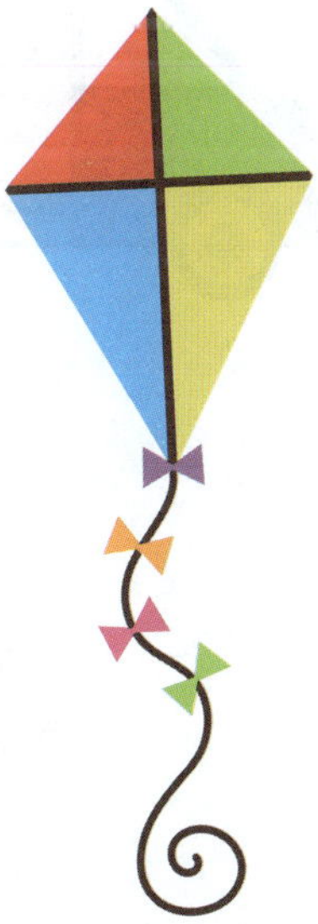

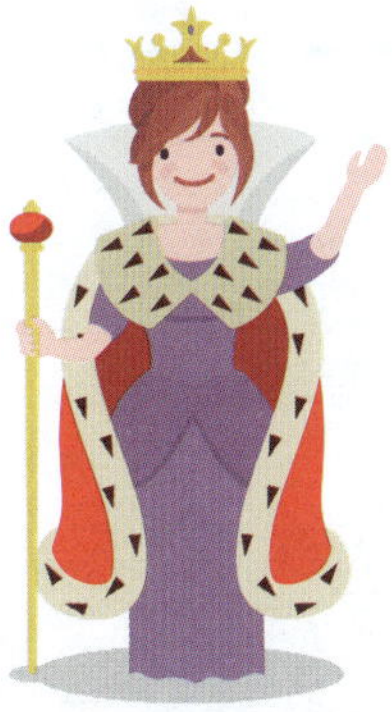

How do you feel about these pages? Tick ✔ the box next to the face that shows how you feel.

Letters s-z

● Join these letter sounds to the correct picture.

s
t
u
v
w
x
y
z

Reading three-letter words

When we put letter sounds together, we can make words.

- Using sounds, can you sound out each letter and hear a word, then match it to the correct picture?

c a t

d o g

m a n

p e g

- Now try these words.

s u n

b i n

l o g

m a t

How do you feel about these pages? Tick ✔ the box next to the face that shows how you feel.

Number maze

0   1   2   3   4   5   6   7   8   9   10

- Join the dots in the correct number order so that the fire engine can continue down the road.

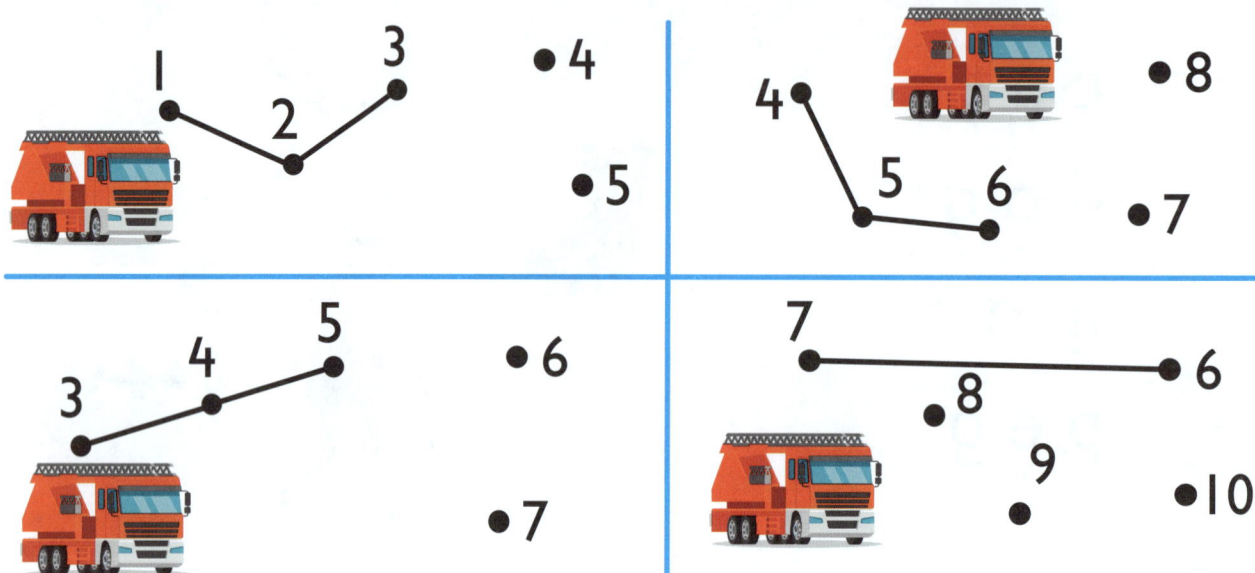

- Fill in the missing numbers in the fire ladder. In each ladder, colour the highest number red and the lowest number green.

When giving a number of things to your child, like 6 grapes or 2 biscuits, say 'Can you take 6 grapes?' or 'Can you take 2 biscuits?'. If they get it wrong, try not to correct, just start again with you counting the correct number of items.

Counting

● How many dinosaurs are in each box? Can you find the two boxes that have the same number? Join them together.

● Look at the dinosaurs and their leaves.
Circle which dinosaur has the most leaves.
Cross out which dinosaur has the least leaves.

Shapes

- Draw the shape and say the name of the shape.

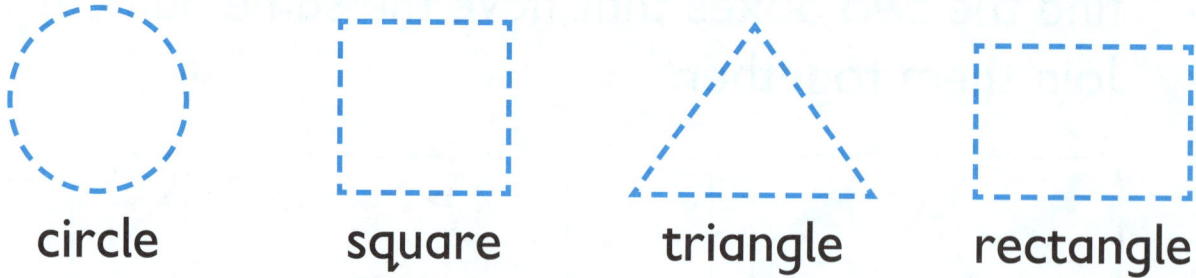

circle   square   triangle   rectangle

- Now practise drawing the shapes.

- Draw the shapes. What are the shapes called? Say the names.

oval   heart   diamond

- Now practise drawing the shapes.

- Can you match the shape to the object?

- Can you look in an old magazine or catalogue and find some shapes to cut out? Stick your shapes here.

My shapes sticking picture

How do you feel about these pages? Tick ✔ the box next to the face that shows how you feel.

Jobs people do

There are lots of different jobs that people do. One day, when you are older, you will be able to choose a job to do.

- Look at the people below. Can you match them to the things they use in their jobs?

Dominic and Jenny are artists.

Tamsin and James are mechanics.

Vivek and Rasena are doctors.

Jodie and Pavel are ballet dancers.

Miss Clay and Mr Wadmore are teachers.

Sara and Stuart are police officers.

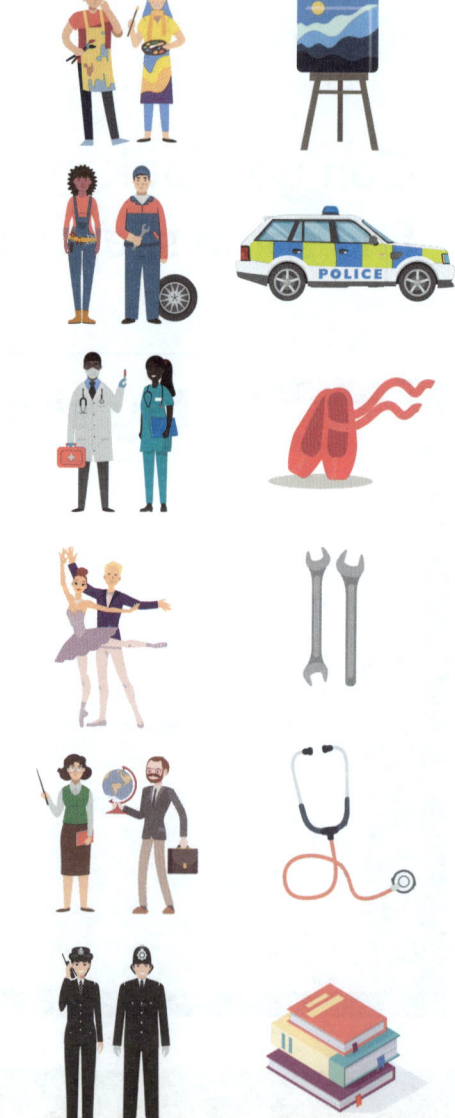

Children love hearing about what people do for their jobs and love role-playing. It is very important to let them role-play and rehearse future roles. Talk about jobs you do or would like to do, or you may have friends that can talk about their jobs.

Pets

Follow the maze to help the pets reach their homes.

How do you feel about these pages? Tick ✔ the box next to the face that shows how you feel.

 ☐ ☐ ☐

Dinosaurs

No dinosaurs live in the world today as they are all extinct.

- Colour the dinosaurs and match them to their skeletons.

Tyrannosaurus Rex

Diplodocus

Stegosaurus

Triceratops

Coelophysis

- There is some food by each dinosaur. Some eat meat, so colour this food red . Others only eat plants, so colour this food green .

- This is a Pterodactyl. It was a flying reptile. It lived and died out at the same time as the dinosaurs. Colour the Pterodactyl and its food.

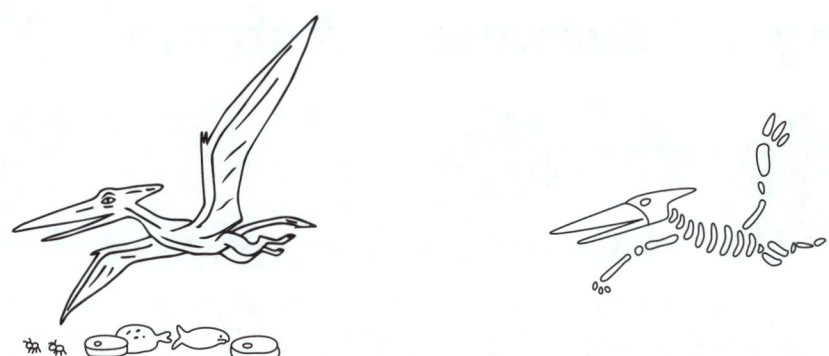

- The ancestors of these reptiles and fish lived when the dinosaurs were alive. We can still see these today. Can you colour them and guess what they are?

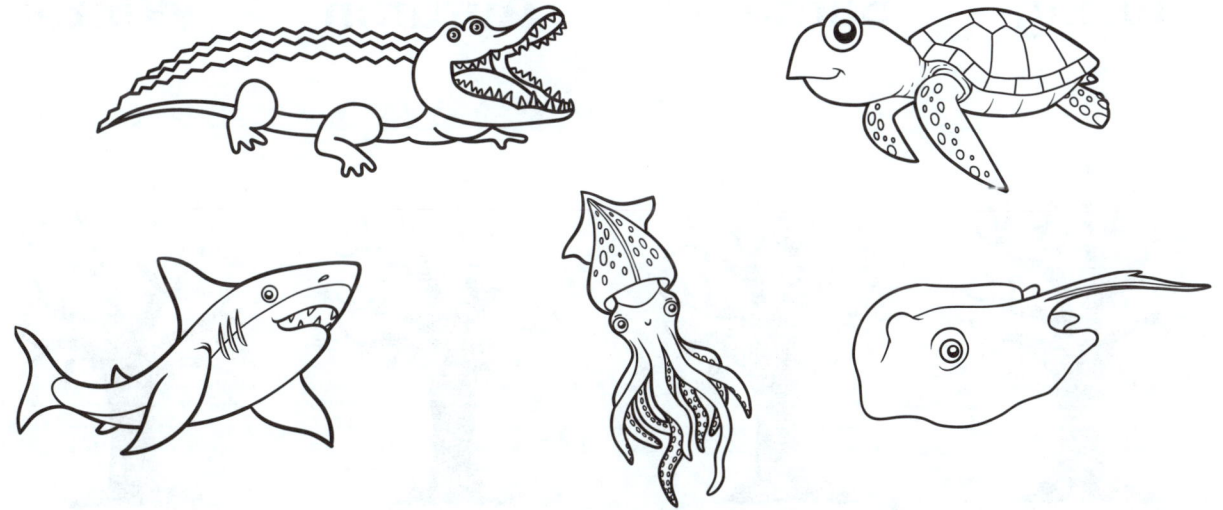

No one knows exactly why all the dinosaurs died out and these reptiles and fish lived.

Seasons

There are four seasons in a year.

Spring	Summer	Autumn	Winter

- Can you add leaves to the trees to match the season? Think about the colour of the leaves in each season. In spring and summer some trees have flowers too.

Spring	Summer	Autumn	Winter

- Can you draw a big circle round your favourite season?

As seasons change, talk about what is happening as you see subtle changes. More people wearing coats or leaves changing colour and falling off trees. More lights are switched on earlier as the days are shorter.

Life cycles

- Write numbers 1, 2, 3 or 4 next to the pictures to put the life cycle of a frog in the right order. Think carefully about which one comes first.

- Now can you do the same for the life cycle of a butterfly? Write, 1, 2, 3 and 4.

How do you feel about these pages? Tick ✔ the box next to the face that shows how you feel.

Weather

● Match each person to the correct weather picture.

● Look outside. What is the weather like today? Tick ✔ which picture is similar to the weather outside now. Put a cross ✗ in the box under the weather you had yesterday.

Children love watching weather reports on television. Involve them in looking at the weather forecast in the newspaper or online when you are planning your day, especially if your activity depends on the weather.

In different types of weather, we do different activities. Match the pictures to activities the weather makes possible.

  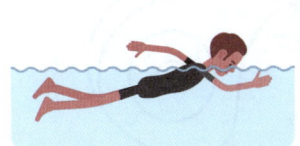 

Sometimes when different weathers mix together, special things happen. Circle the right result and cross ✗ the wrong picture.

Colours

- Copy the colours to finish each butterfly.

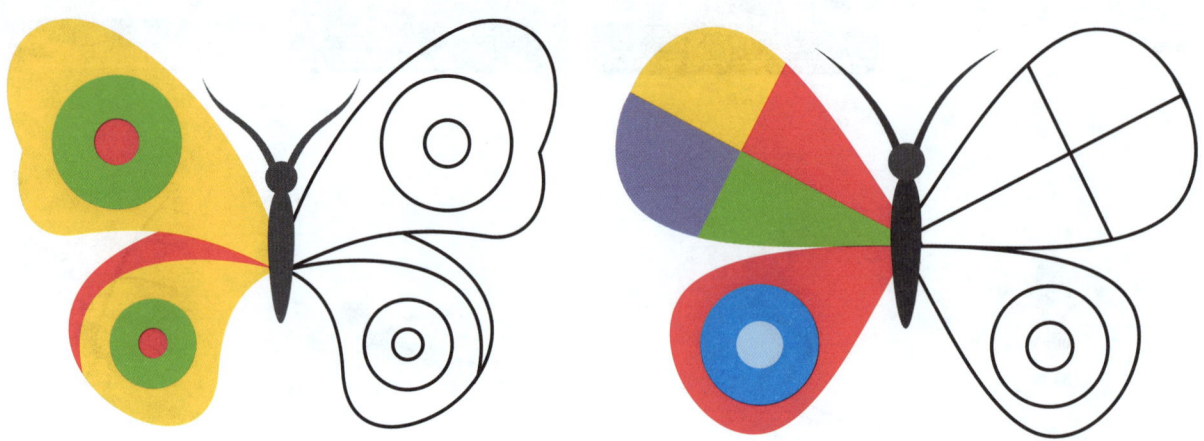

- There are some pictures below with the colours missing. Can you think what colour should be there and fill it in?

Use colour and texture in everyday language. 'Adil, look at the yellow flower', or 'Lewis, this cup is made of plastic and this is made of glass'.

Texture and materials

- Follow the zigzags to join the original material to the object made from it.

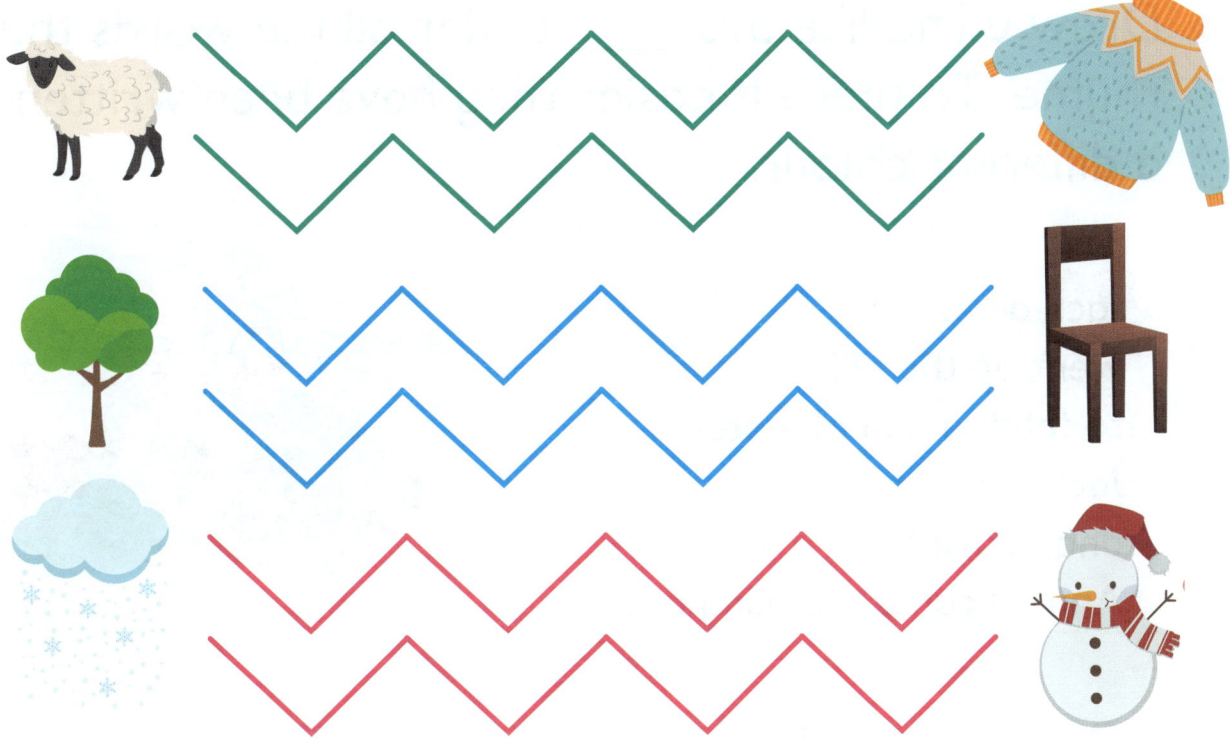

- In the pictures below:

    Colour the rough thing blue.
    Colour the smooth thing red.
    Colour the spiky thing green.
    Colour the soft thing yellow.

How do you feel about these pages? Tick ✔ the box next to the face that shows how you feel.

🔴 ☐   😐 ☐   🟢 ☐

Songs

- Sing the songs below. Ask someone to help if you don't know the tune.
- Draw a line like this _____ under all the words that rhyme. To make it easier they have been written in a different colour.

Jack and Jill
went up the hill
to fetch a pail of water
Jack fell down
and broke his crown
And Jill came tumbling after.

Old Mother Hubbard
Went to the cupboard
To get her poor doggie a bone,
When she got there
The cupboard was bare
So the poor little doggie had none.

It's raining, it's pouring
The old man is snoring
He went to bed
and he bumped his head
And couldn't get up in the morning.

Point out words that are similar, like 'Jill' and 'hill', and discuss how by changing one letter the whole word changes. For example, 'mill', 'bill', 'bell', 'fell'. Can you list more and discuss them together?

Stories

● Look at the pictures below. Can you tell the story?

1

2

3

4

5

How do you feel about these pages? Tick ✔ the box next to the face that shows how you feel.

 ☐ ☐ ☐

Answers

Page 4

Child's self-portrait

Child's food drawings

Page 5

Child's drawing of their family

Child's drawing of their home

Page 6

Page 7

Child to tick the activities they do often

Page 8

Child's decorated eggs

Child to join the dots

Page 9

Child to trace the lines and colour the picture

Page 10

write – pencil

cut paper – scissors

cut wood – saw

make tea – kettle

make a car go – petrol pump

Page 11

Page 12

Page 13

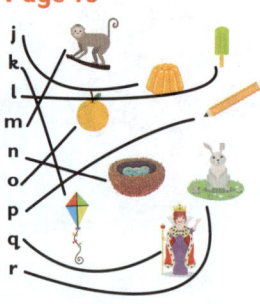

Page 14

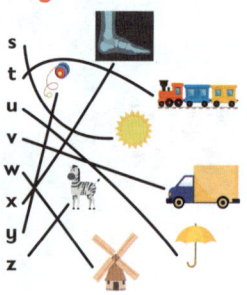

Page 15

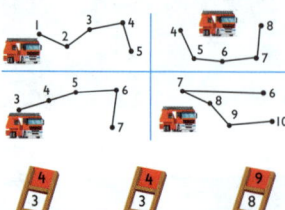

Page 16

Page 17

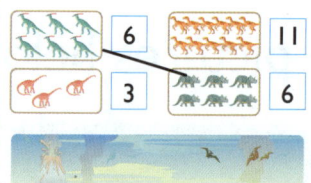

Page 18

Child's dot-to-dot shapes

Page 19

Child's shapes from magazines

Page 20

Page 21

Child's completed maze

Page 22

Child to colour the dinosaurs

Page 23

Child to colour the Pterodactyl and its food

Child to colour the reptiles and fish

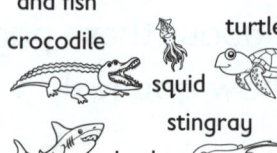

crocodile   turtle

squid

stingray

shark

Page 24

Child to add leaves to trees and circle their favourite season

Page 25

Page 26

Child to tick today's weather and cross yesterday's weather

Page 27

Page 28

Child to complete the butterflies

Page 29

Child to draw lines

Page 30

Jill, hill;
down, crown

Hubbard, cupboard;
there, bare

pouring, snoring;
bed, head

Page 31

Child to tell the story in their own words